Frogs Live on Logs

Melvin and Gilda Berger

SCHOLASTIC INC.

New York   Toronto   London   Auckland   Sydney
Mexico City   New Delhi   Hong Kong   Buenos Aires

Photographs: Cover: Kenneth H. Thomas/Photo Researchers, New York; p. 1: Scott Camazine/Photo Researchers; p. 3: A. B. Sheldon/Dembinsky Photo Associates, Owosso, MI; p. 4: Sharon Cummings/Dembinsky Photo Associates; p. 5: Phil McLean/Holt Studios Int'l/Photo Researchers; p. 6: John Serrao/Photo Researchers; p. 7: Michael Mosby/Bruce Coleman, Inc., New York; p. 8: Andy Harmer/Science Photo Library/Photo Researchers; p. 9: Stephen Dalton/Photo Researchers; p. 10: E. R. Degginger/Bruce Coleman, Inc; p. 11: Dr. Paul A. Zahl/Photo Researchers; p. 12: Scott Camazine/Photo Researchers; p. 13: Michael P. Gadomski/Photo Researchers; p. 14: Eastcott/Momatiuk/ Photo Researchers; p. 15: Karl H. Switak/Photo Researchers; p. 16: Gregory G. Dimijian/Photo Researchers.

Book design by Annette Cyr

ISBN 0-439-47176-1

12 11 10 9 8 7   4 5 6 7 8/0

Printed in the U.S.A.
First printing, January 2003

Frogs live on logs.

Frogs live on land and in water.

All frogs lay eggs in water.

Some frogs live mostly on land.

Some frogs live mostly in water.

Land frogs are good jumpers.

Land frogs have big,
strong back legs.

Water frogs are good swimmers.

Water frogs have skin
between their toes.

Frogs live in trees.

Tree frogs are good climbers.

Frogs live in the ground.

Ground frogs are good diggers.

Can you spot the frog?